MW01166673

VIBRANT
Ann Arbor
A Color Portrait

Rosalie Savarino Edwards, editor and publisher

Photographs by Doris Kays Kraushaar

Supplemental photographs by Robert Kalmbach

*A*nn Arbor is many cities: a small, friendly town with big city sophistication; a medical and high-tech research center nestled in a sleepy rural setting; a close-knit community of neighborhoods and churches that is also rich in ethnic cultures.

Home to the University of Michigan, Ann Arbor is a tree-filled city small enough to bike across in an afternoon yet diverse enough to attract world-class performing artists, support myriad gourmet restaurants, and host a nationally recognized art fair.

Join a hundred thousand avid U-M football fans on a sunny fall Saturday or savor the sights and smells at the Farmers' Market. Listen to a lecture, visit a museum, or browse in some of the finest bookstores in the country. Shop in the unique art galleries and boutiques, or sip cappuccino and people-watch at an outdoor cafe.

There are many Ann Arbors. Take your pick and enjoy.

Rosalie S. Edwards

Rosalie Savarino Edwards

Contents

Copyright © 1995 by R. S. Edwards and J. W. Edwards Publishing, Inc.
Photographs copyright © by Doris Kays Kraushaar and Robert Kalmbach
All rights reserved
ISBN 1-886569-05-3
Manufactured in the United States of America
Edwards Brothers, Inc., Ann Arbor, Michigan
Design by Ron Fraker

Front cover: View of State Street from North University Street.
Back cover: The University of Michigan Law Library.
All photographs by Doris Kays Kraushaar (unless otherwise credited).

Photo by Robert Kalmbach

All proceeds benefit Ann Arbor Area Community Foundation.

Around Town

Zingerman's Deli

Dining on Main Street

Main Street during the holidays

Wall of Writers (Woody Allen, Edgar Allen Poe, Hermann Hess, Franz Kafka, Anais Nin),
Liberty at State street

Washtenaw Dairy

West Park

Farmers' Market

Escoffier

Fleetwood Diner

Sweet Lorraine's

Bistro restaurant

Gandy Dancer restaurant (former railway station)

Kerrytown patio

Borders Books & Music

After words bookstore

Drake's Sandwich Shop

Blimpy Burger restaurant
(winter display)

Dobson–McOmber Insurance office building

Domino's world headquarters

St. Andrews Episcopal Church

The Parker barn

St. Joseph Mercy Hospital

Photo by Lance Burghardt

Great Lakes Bancorp

Events

Summer Festival "Top of the Park" entertainment

Art Fair

Aerial view of State Street during Art Fair

Photo by Robert Kalmbach

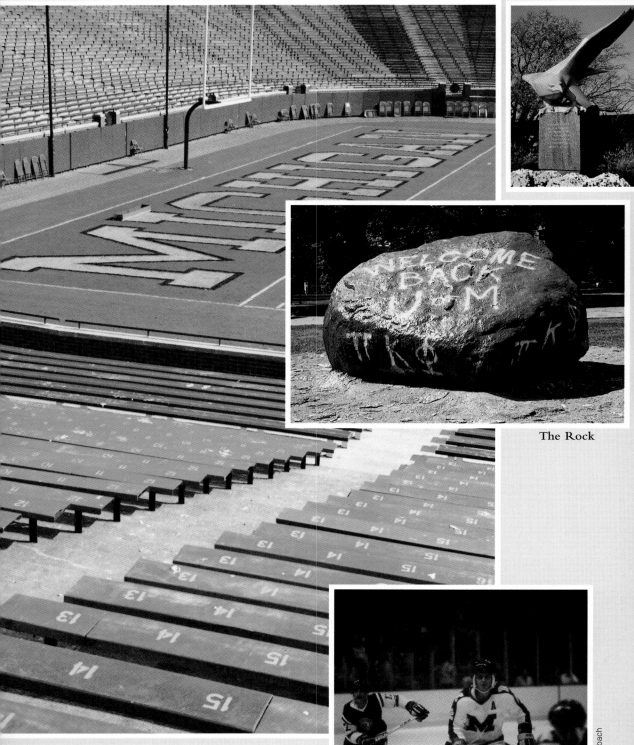

Sculpture by Marshall Fredericks honoring U-M athletes killed in WWII

The Rock

Photo by Robert Kalmbach

Photo by Robert Kalmbach

Photo by Robert Kalmbach

Photo by Robert Kalmbach

Kerrytown Concert House

Michigan Theater

Political rally on campus

Photo by Robert Kalmbach

Kiosk at Hill Auditorium

Power Center for the Performing Arts

Lydia Mendelssohn Theatre

Ann Arbor Civic Theatre production

Parks and
Gardens

West Park Band Concert

Matthaei Botanical Gardens

Gallup Park

Barton Pond

Canoeing on the Huron River

Island Park pavilion

Nichols Arboretum

Museums

Kelsey Museum, University of Michigan

Museum of Art, University of Michigan *(above and below)*

Cobblestone Farm (a living farm museum built in 1844)
(above and right)

Ann Arbor Hands-On Museum, former fire
station *(left and right)*

Exhibit Museum, University of Michigan
(above and left)

Kempf House (Greek Revival house built in 1853)

Campus

Law Library

Law School Courtyard

View of Law Quad with president's house in foreground

West Engineering Building

The Shapiro Library (formerly Undergraduate Library)

(Cube) kinetic sculpture by Bernard Rosenthal at Regents Plaza

Sunday Morning in Deep Waters
fountain by Carl Millus

Photo by Robert Kalmbach

Burton Memorial Tower and Ingalls Mall

Horace H. Rackham School of Graduate Studies

Angel Hall Computing Site
"computer cathedral"

Angell Hall

Michigan Union

Michigan League

Hill Auditorium

Connector between U Hospital and Towsley Center University Hospitals

Entrance to A. Alfred Taubman Health Care Center, University of Michigan Hospitals

Academic procession

Gerald R. Ford Library

Willard H. Dow
Chemistry Building

View from eighteenth fairway, U of M golf course

Alumni Center

The Hamilton Fountain, corner of North
University and State streets

William L. Clements Library